Happiness Quotations

Calm During Uncertainty

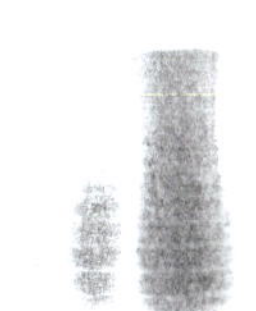

HAPPINESS QUOTATIONS: CALM DURING UNCERTAINTY

ISBN 978-1-63684-918-8
Photographs by Rich Cruse
Written by Erica Marie Glessing
Editor & Photo Curation Isabel Nelson
Cover Design by Vlatko Josifov
Interior Design by Noel Morado

Published by Happy Publishing.
Distributed by Ingram.

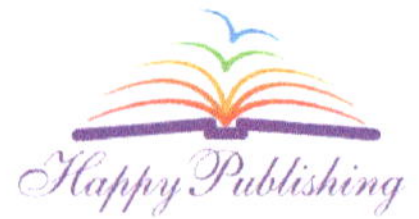

Table of Contents

Be Gentle to You

Be more gentle in your own thoughts about yourself. Be easier and kinder and more loving and cherish this moment, deeply.

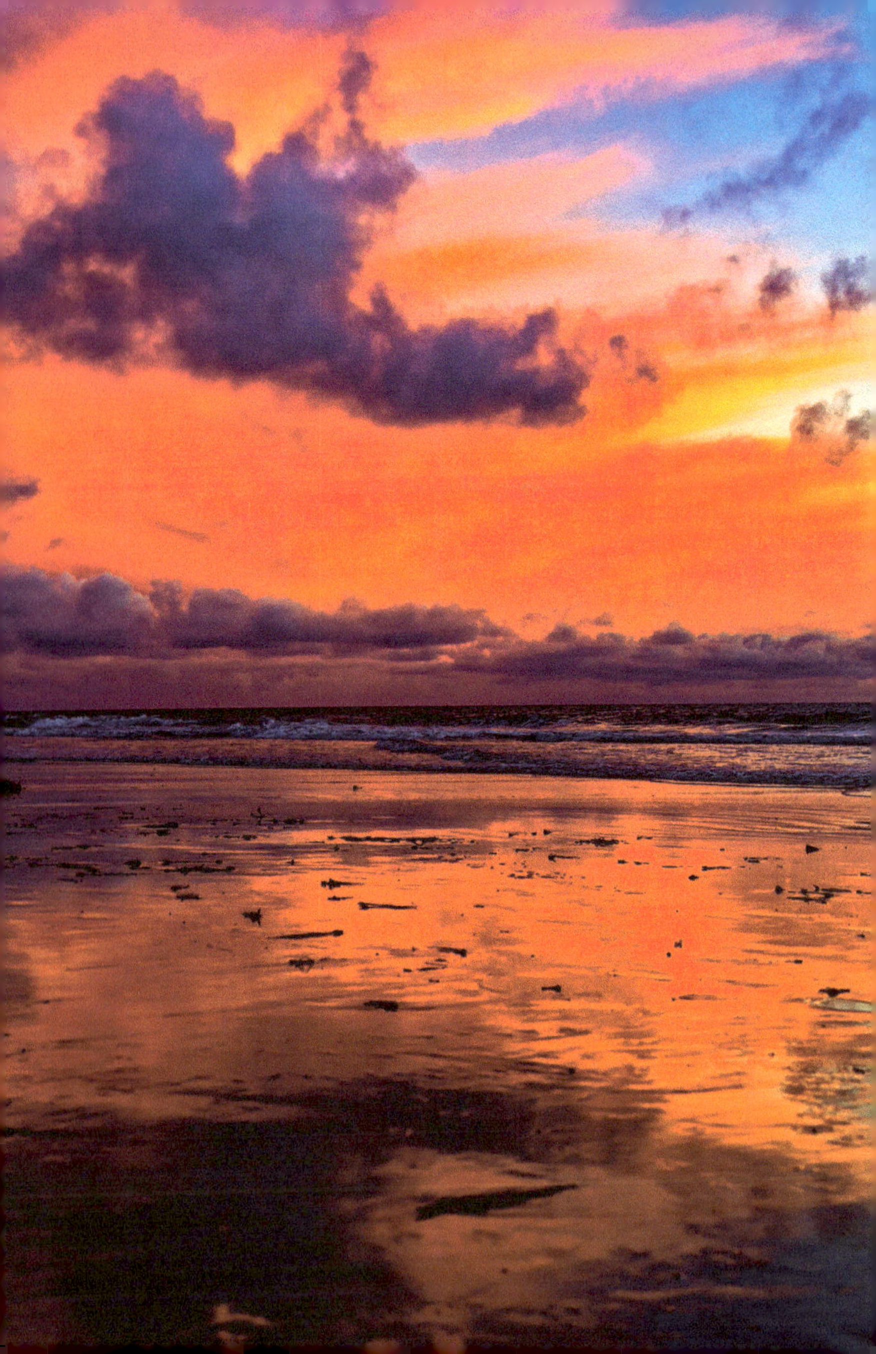

Powerful Opportunities

Powerful challenges create powerful opportunities. You are given challenges and how do you face them? Do you grow? Do you hide? It's not always about how you navigate the good times, sometimes it is about how you navigate the steep climbs.

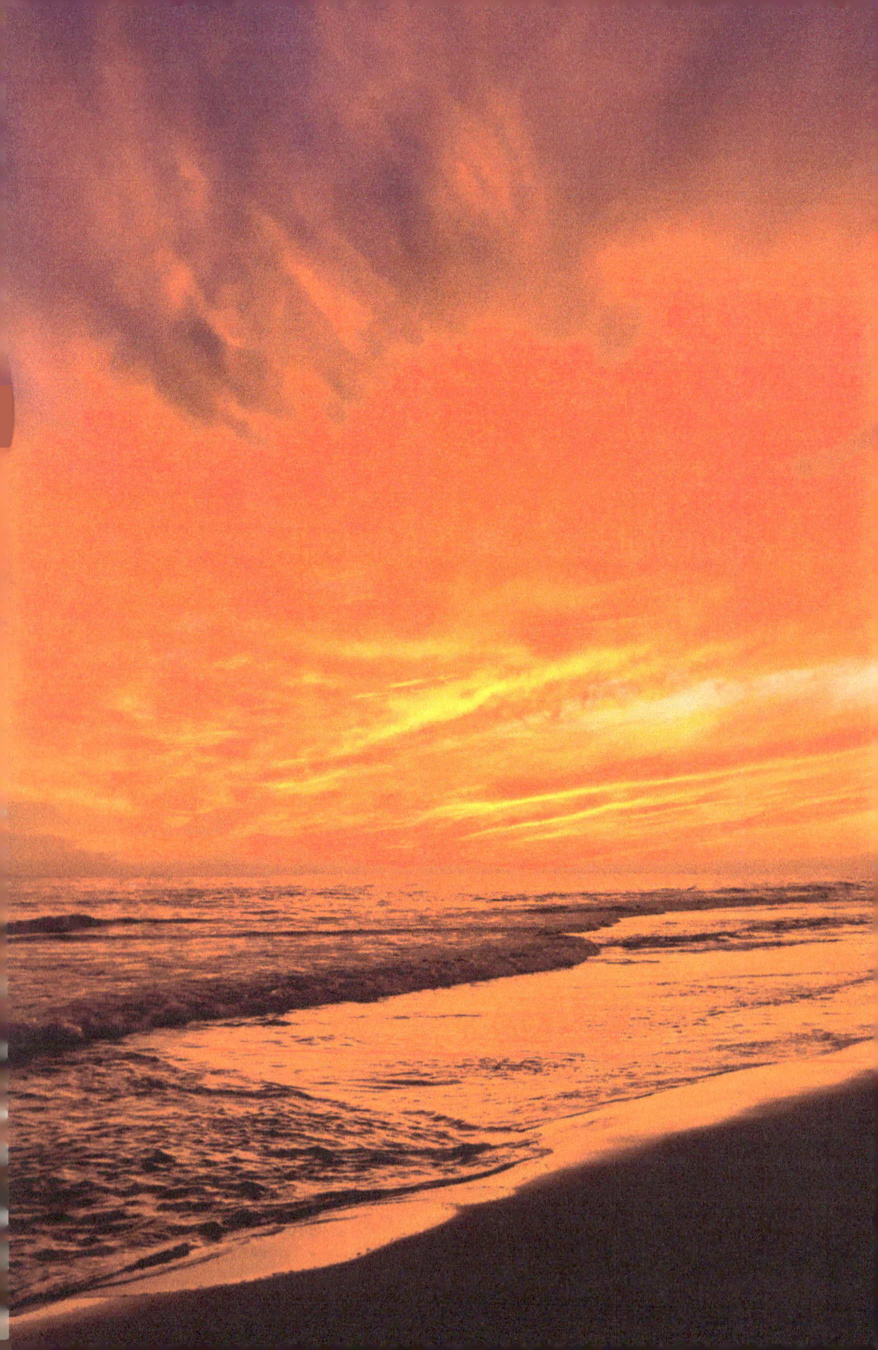

It's Never About You

It is so rarely about you. You think it is about you, when someone else gets upset or has an issue or can't get through a tough time. It's not about you. Let go of that.

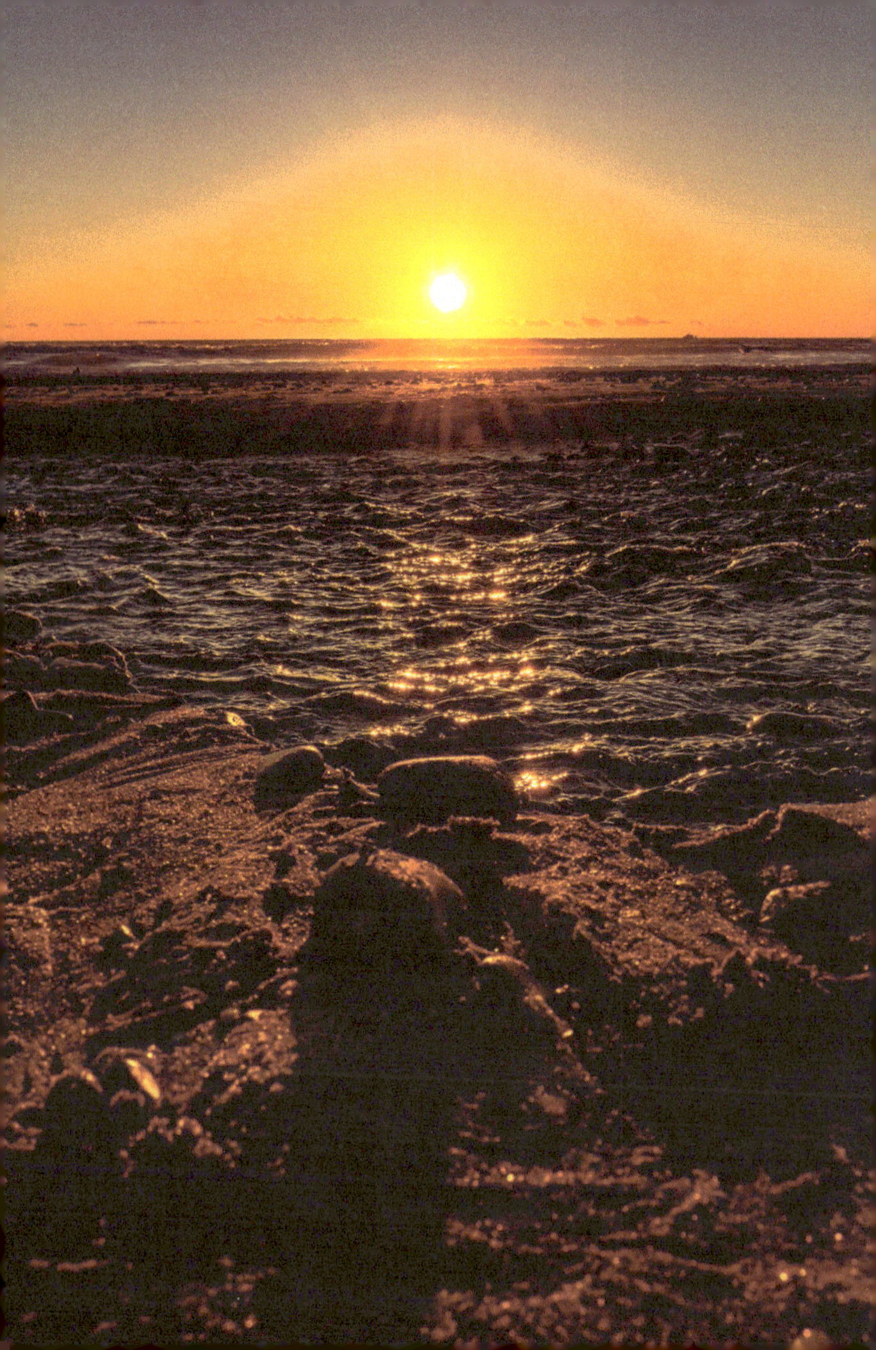

Clear Skies Beckon

Look inside you for clarity. Do not look for answers from others. Do not look for answers where they are not. Open up your heart and ask within. See what happens.

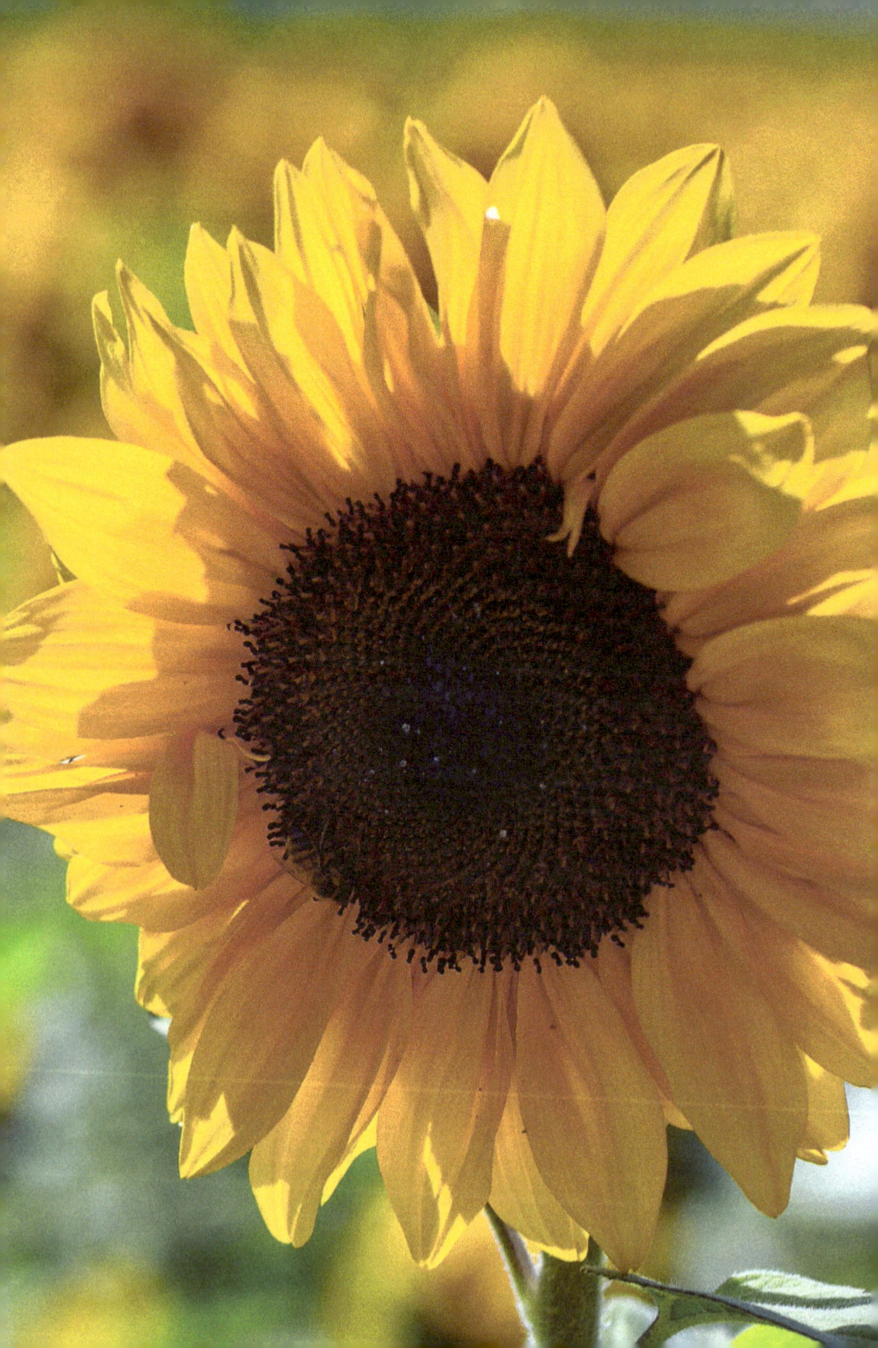

Is All Well, Truly?

You hear "all is well" and you wonder, is this well? Is this all it could be? Is there more? For today, breathe into wellness. What if all is truly well? What if this is what we came here for, to experience this and more. See if you can uncover that knowing 'All is Well' everywhere you go today. Accept this as your birthright.

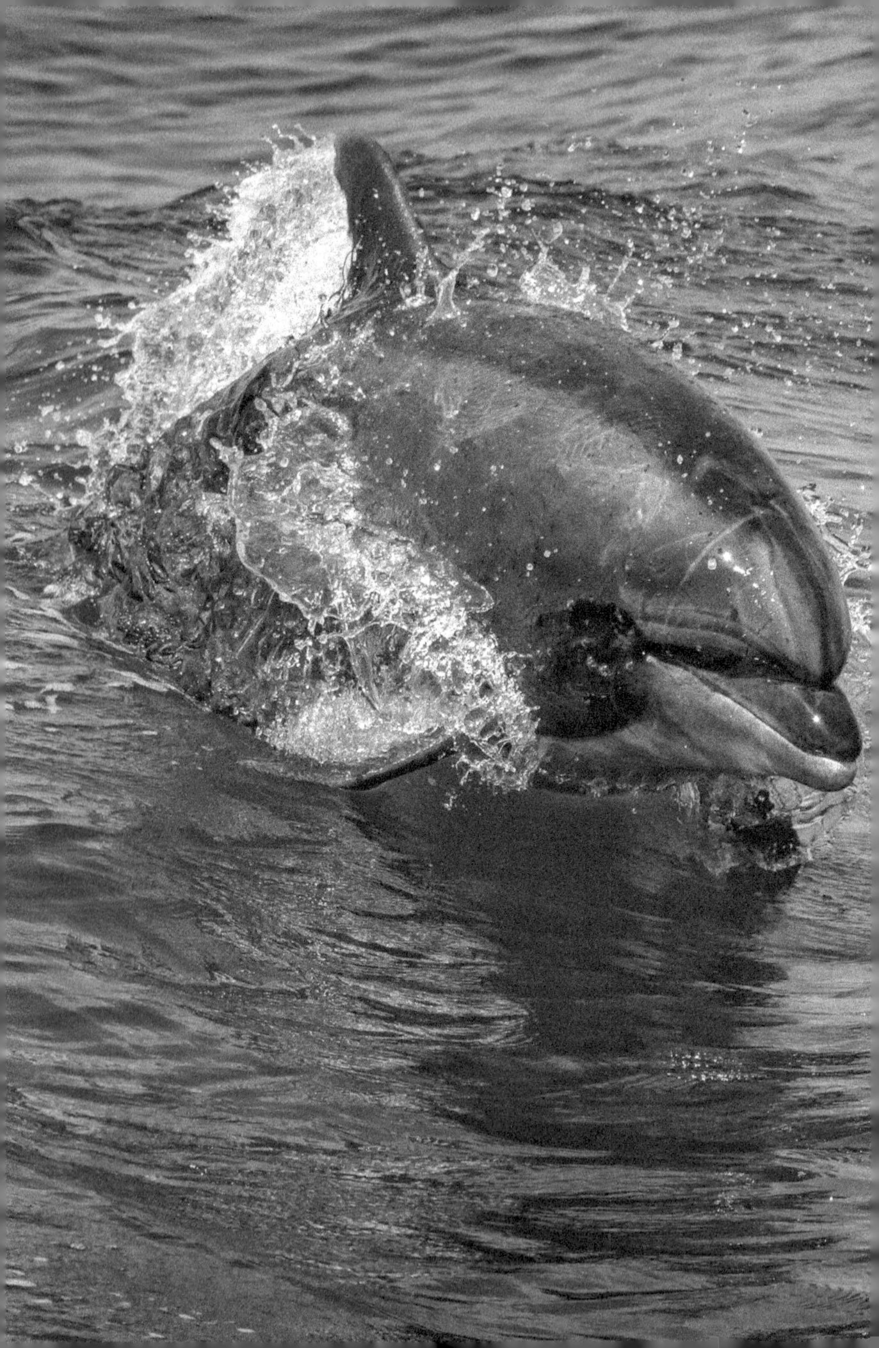

Forgive All

Forgive everyone who did not think you were enough. Forgive everyone who criticized you for anything, ever. Forgive everyone who did not see your beauty. Forgive everyone, perhaps they were not capable of seeing your intense light and gorgeousness.

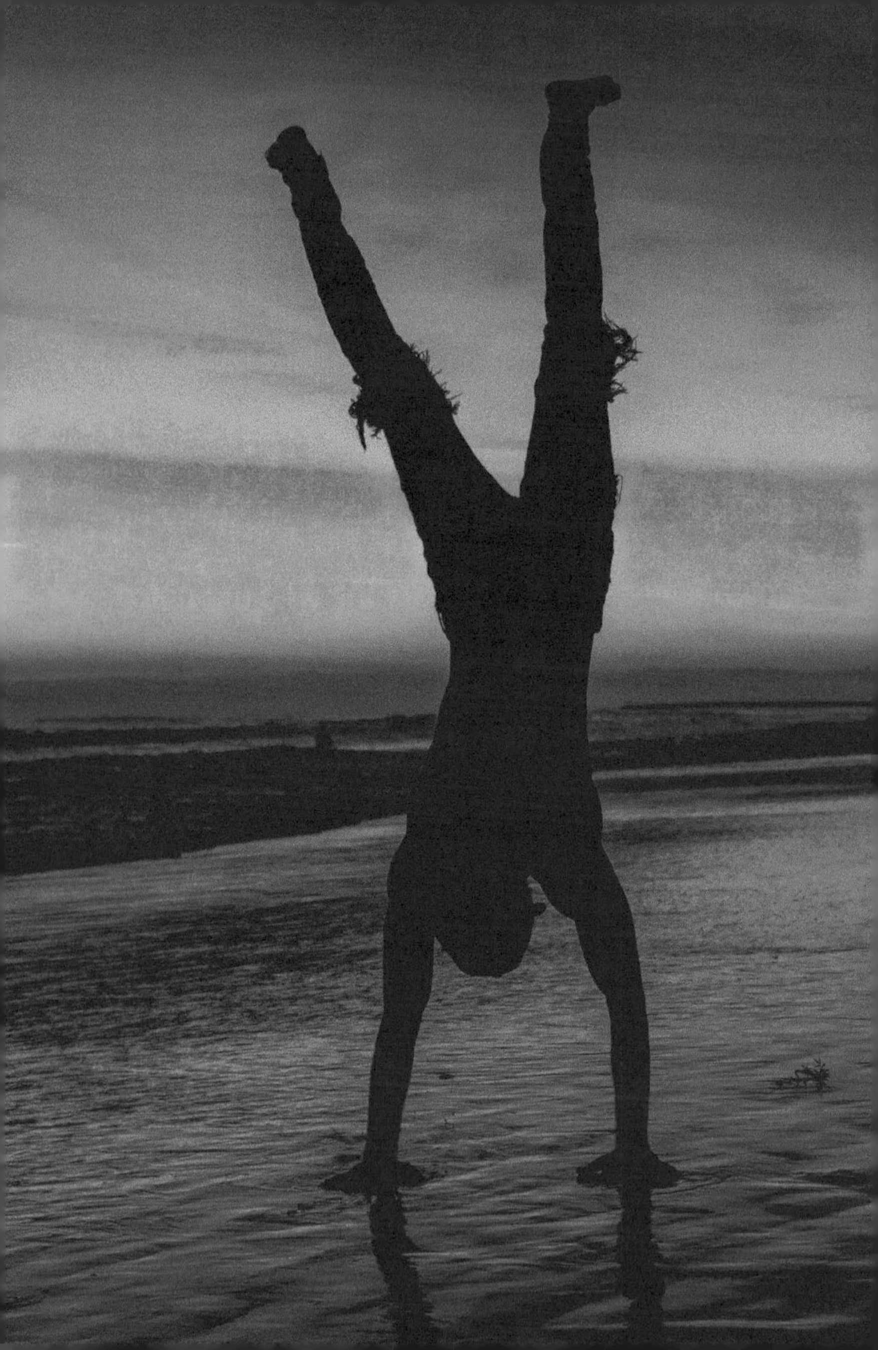

Tune into Your Raw Being

What is your raw energy? What lights you on fire? Get in touch with that space right now, that moment when you are so on fire that not one thing can keep your dream from being true.

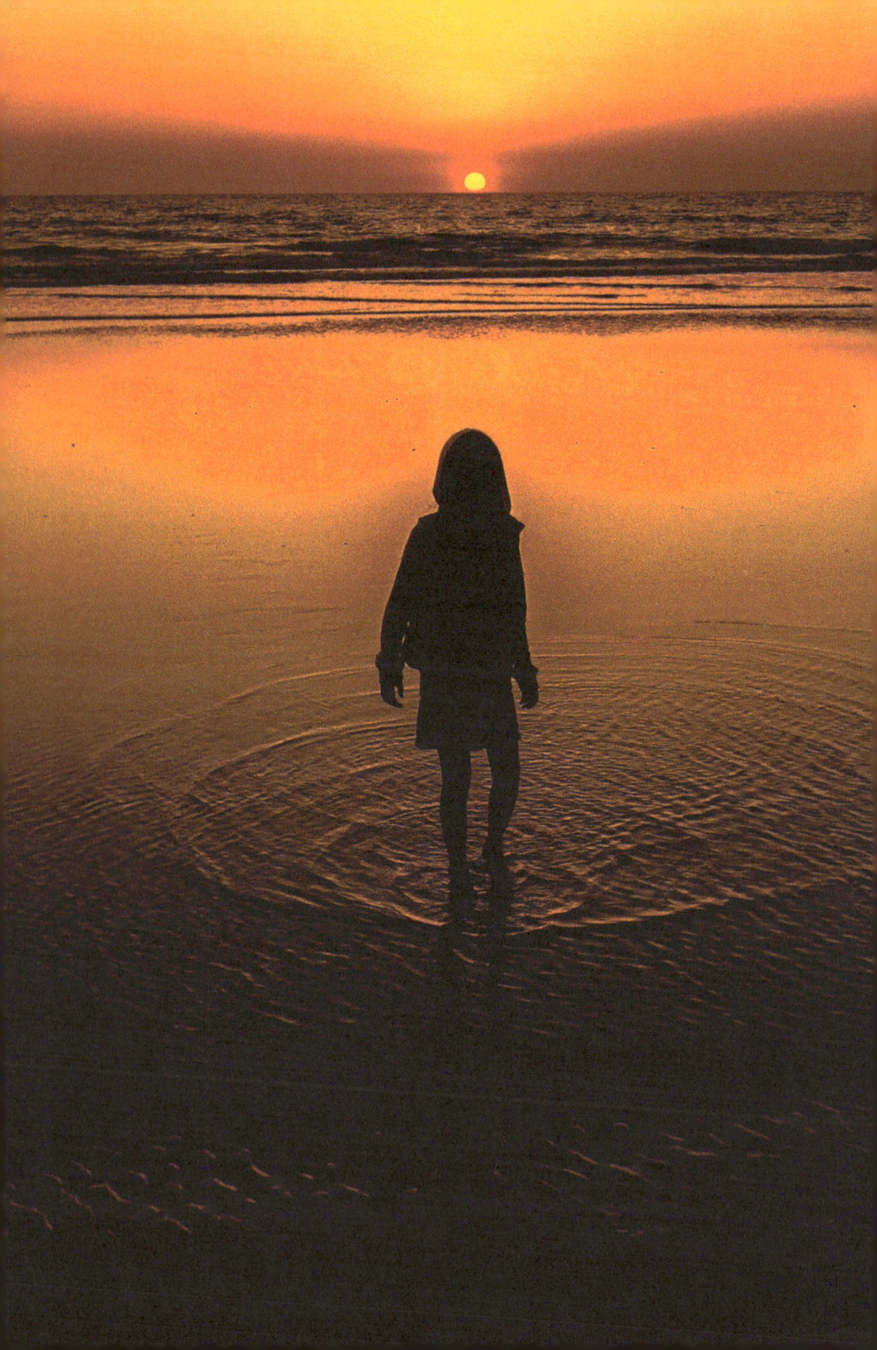

Open Up Your Heart

A new opportunity is always beckoning to allow us to step into bigger shoes, take on new projects, open up our hearts to new sensations of joy, delight, love, truth, honor, everything our heart desires. In this awakening, we are given a chance to experience life with new eyes. Do things differently today. Break the mold. Feel bigger happiness.

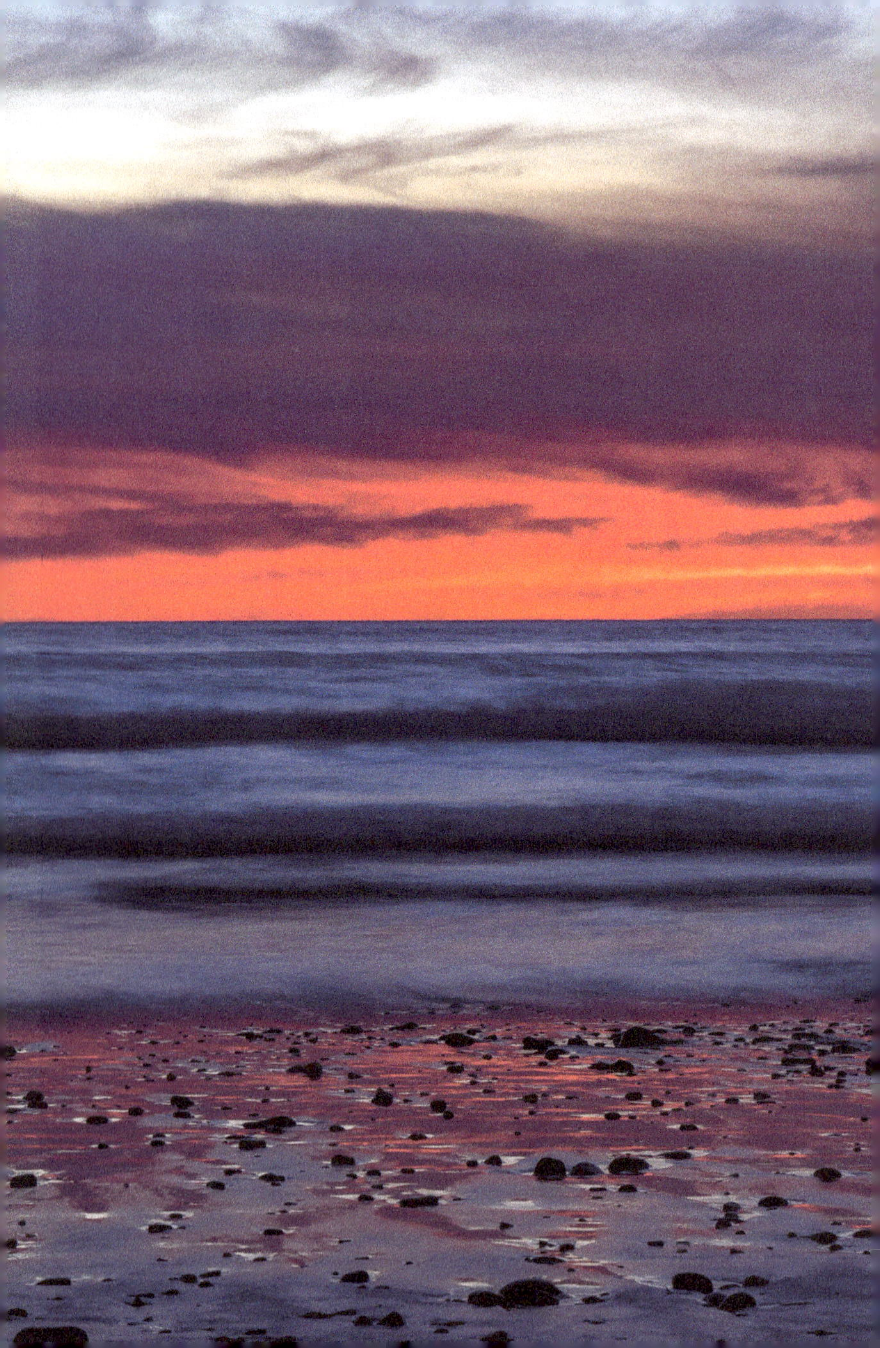

Becoming

We become what we behold. Behold something beautiful today!

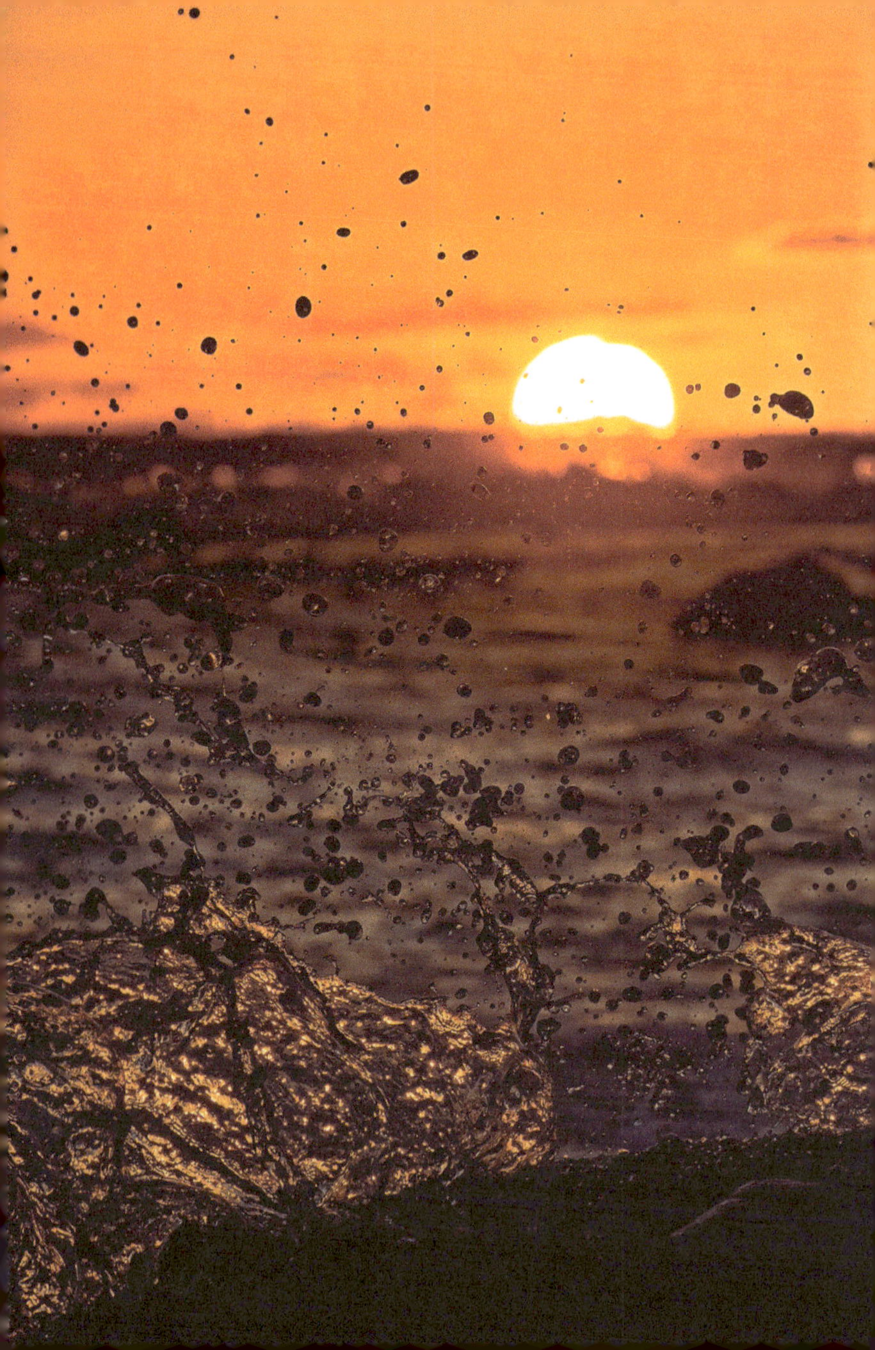

Life is Not Easy

A curveball comes into your life, what is your action? What is your reaction? Does it throw you off course? Does it slap you between the eyebrows? As you tune your fine instrument of beingness, step deeper into your core strength. Step deeper into your ability to navigate any waters. This is true happiness. A curveball becomes a home run.

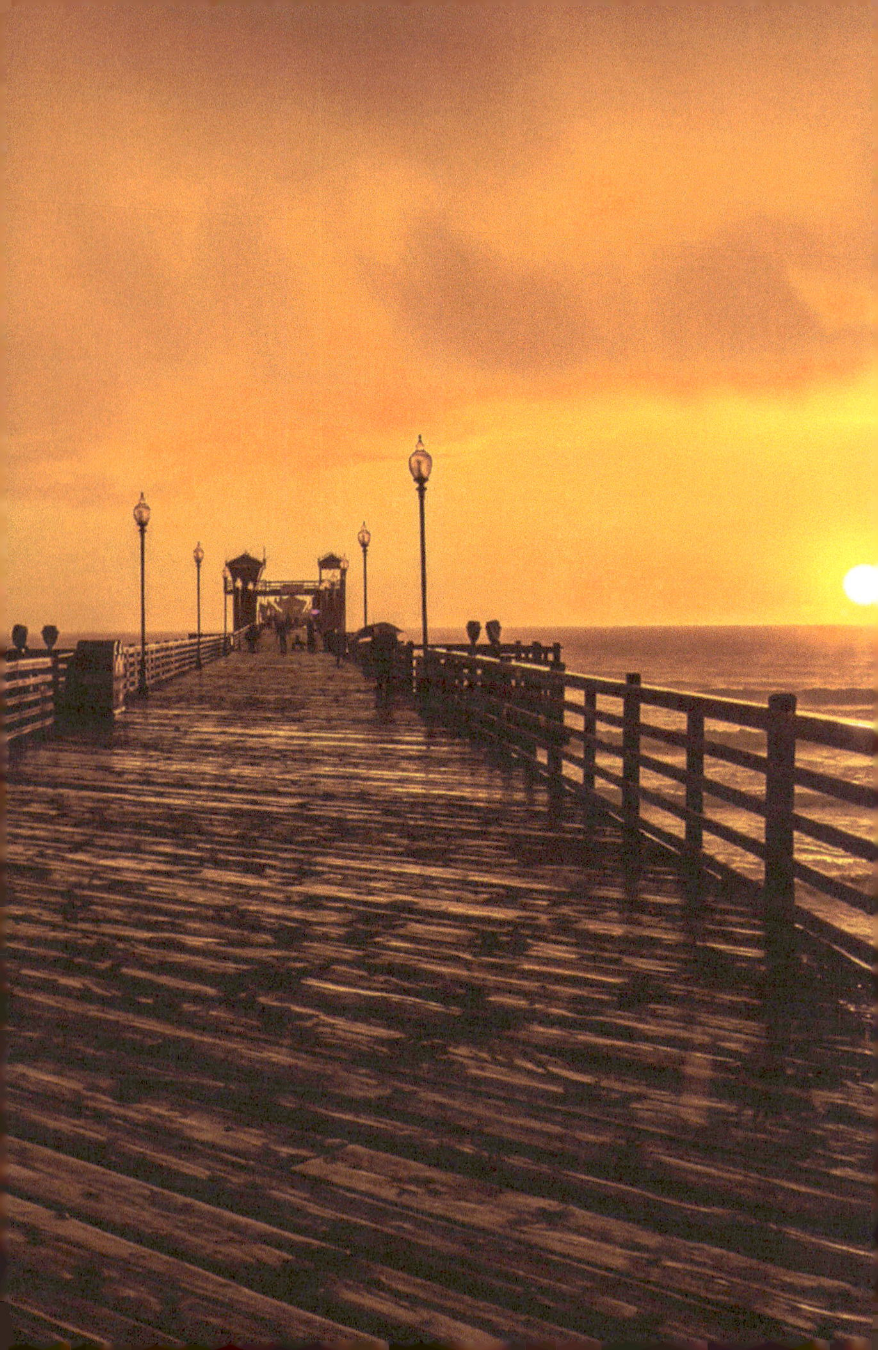

Looking Back at Your Life

When you leave the planet, when you are getting ready to die, what will you treasure most? What will you look back upon in your life? Focus today on the people you love and give them all more love. Notice the relationships you have with your children, parents, husband, lover. How could get deeper into that love? Life is precious, remember to love.

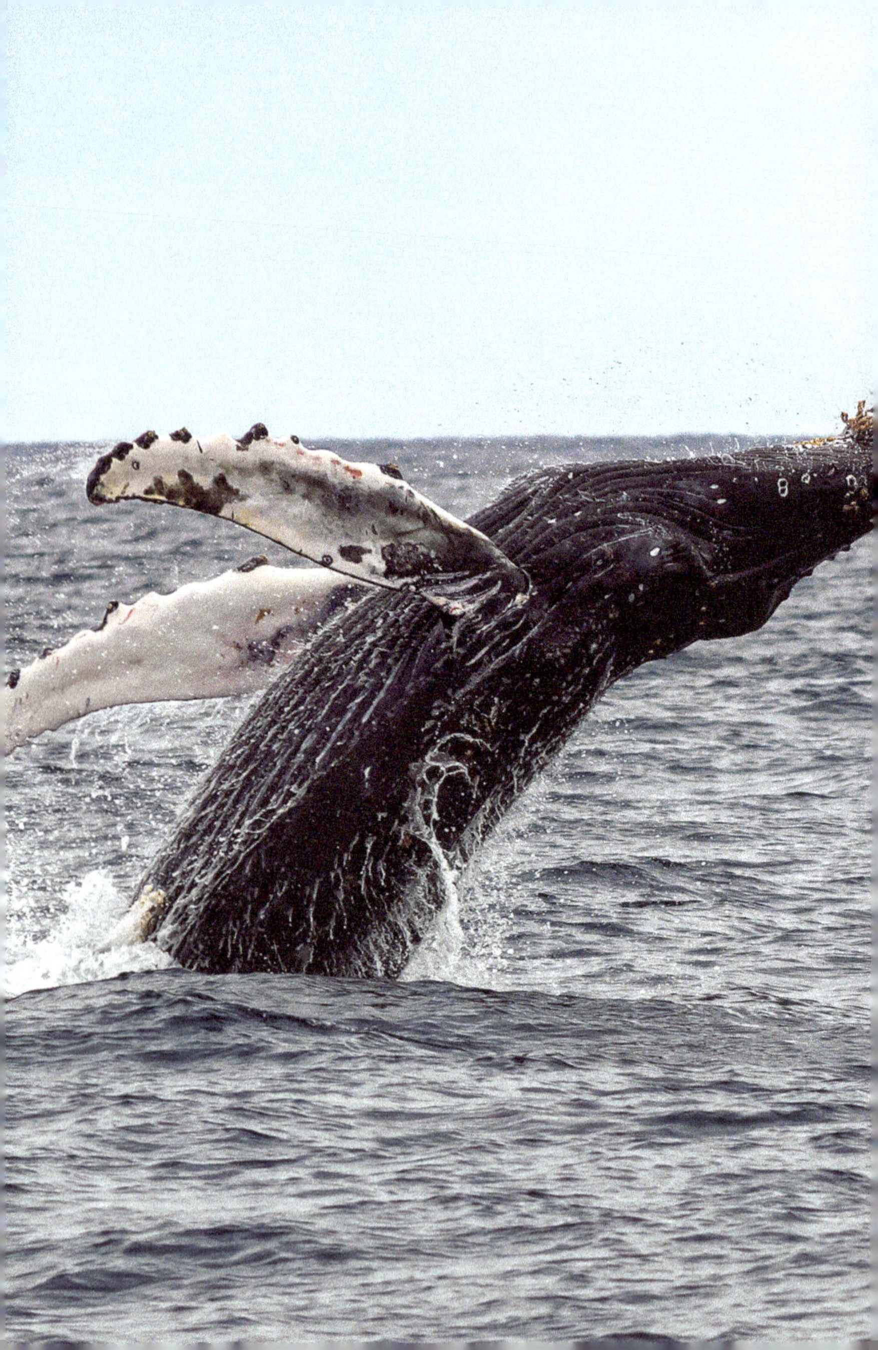

Happiness is Easy

Happiness is not complex. People can be complicated. Remember that happiness feels easy. Your happiest moments are easy, at your fingertips. Choose that.

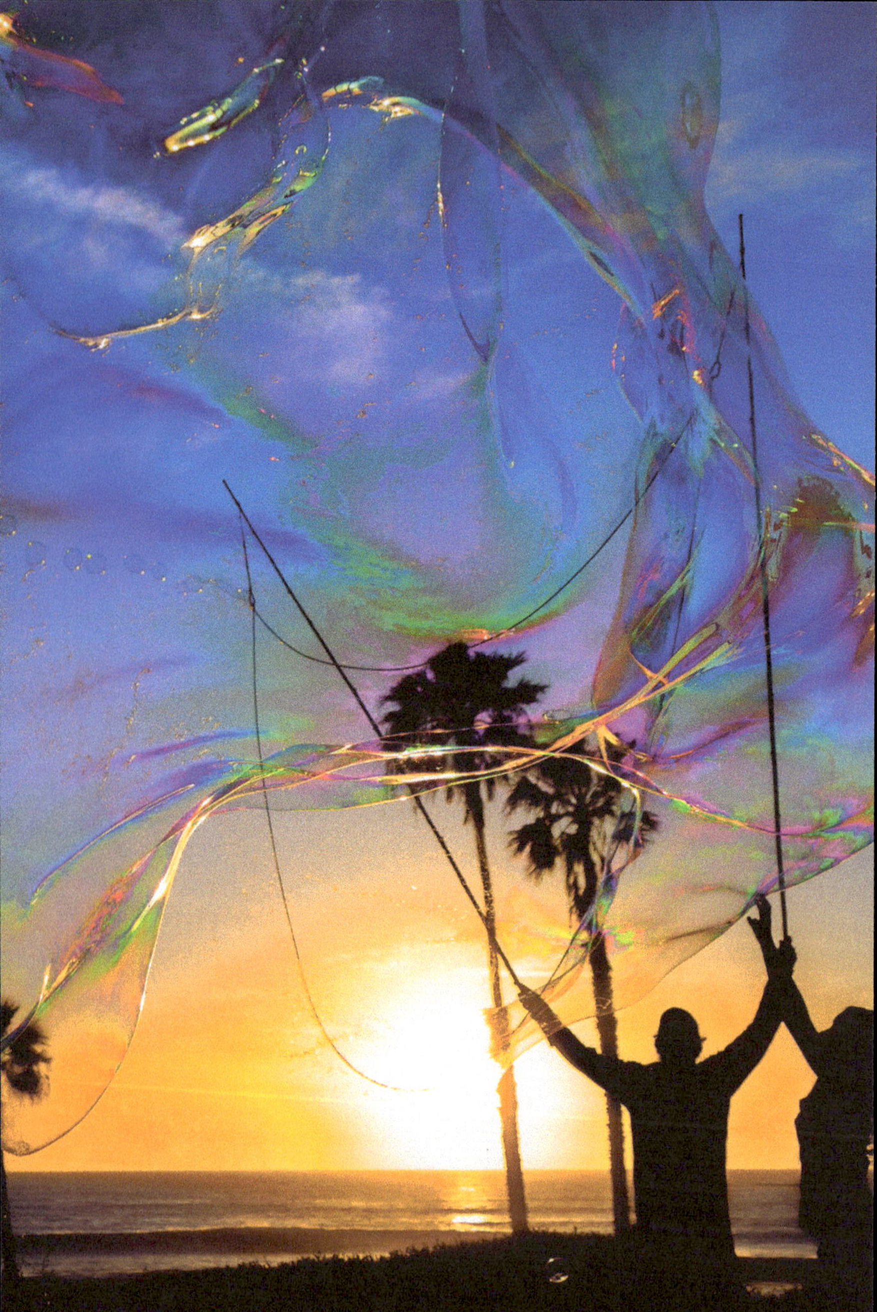

Be Delighted

Let something small make you happy today. Small plus small plus small equals big. Be delighted, easily.

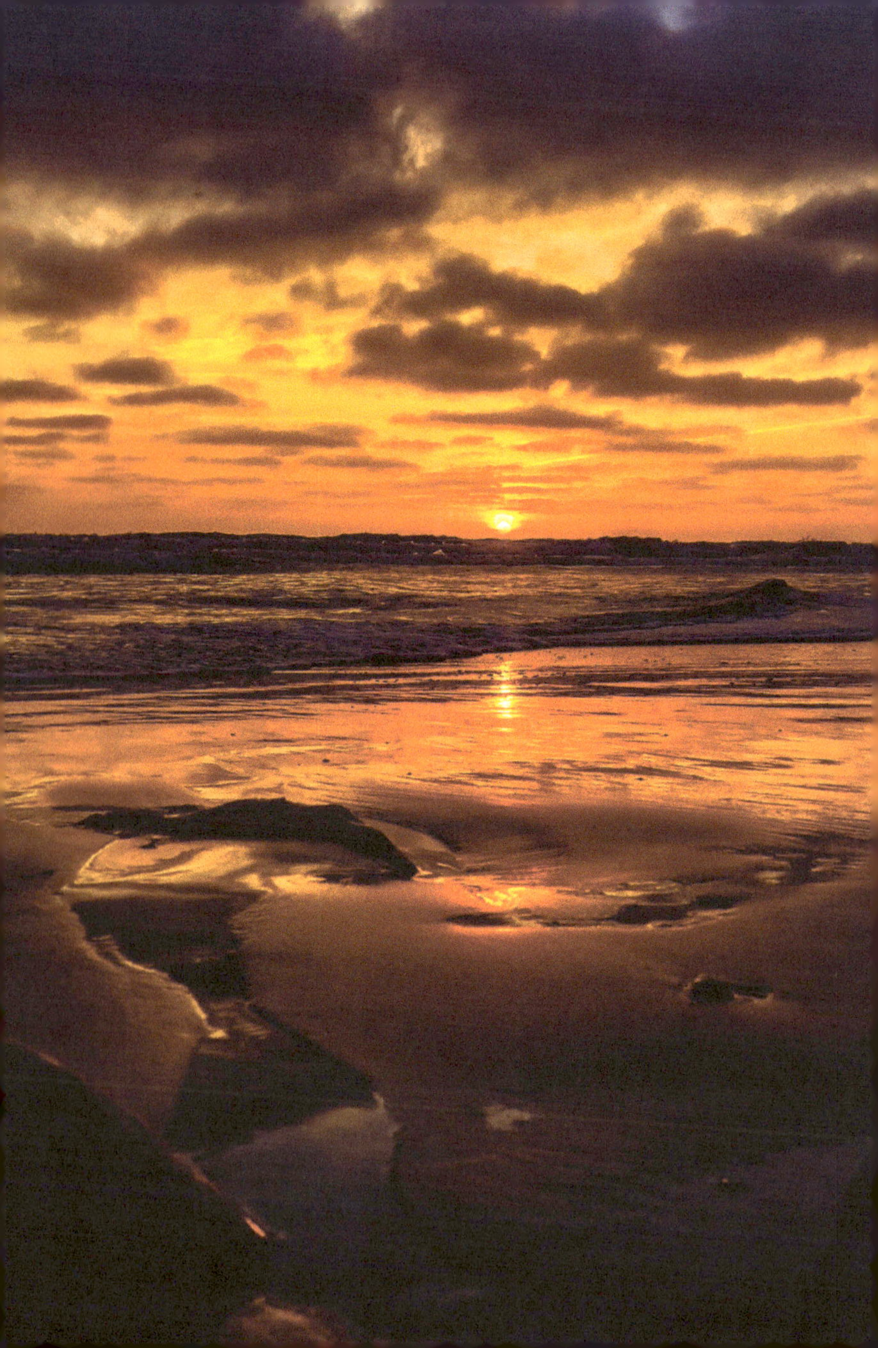

Appreciate Opportunity

Will you recognize opportunity when it is wearing different clothing? When it looks unlike your expectations? Appreciate opportunities today, everywhere, with everyone.

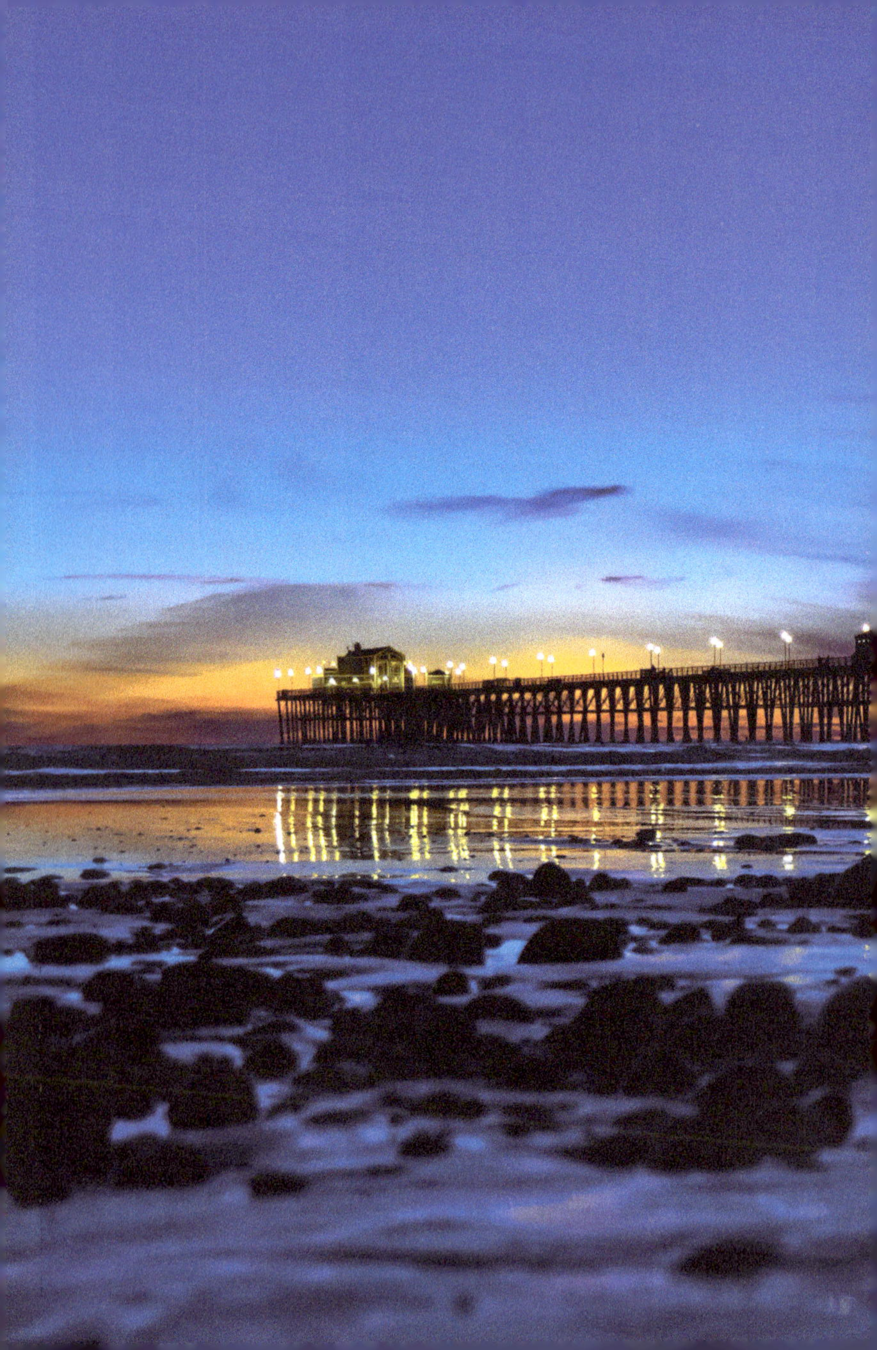

Desire is Life Force

Desire is life force bursting through, wanting to be born. Do not resist your desires, allow them to course through you and bring in new realities. When you choose bigger for yourself, you allow others to do the same. Choose something glorious, for no reason other than you are alive, and you can.

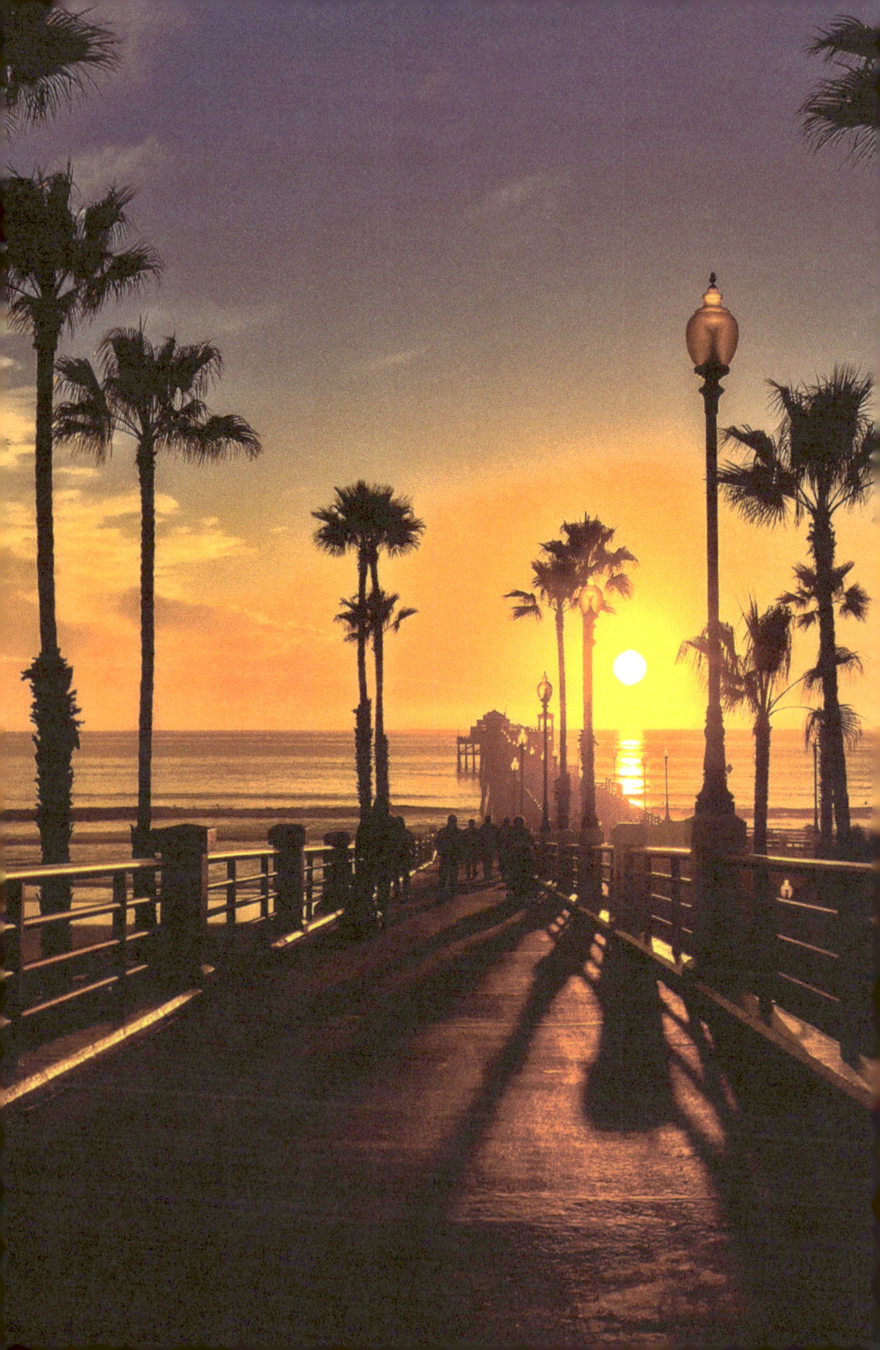

Not Even Looking

Every once in a while, in a rare instant when you stop looking, happiness finds its place in your heart. It flashes in and warms you. Ask for more moments like this.

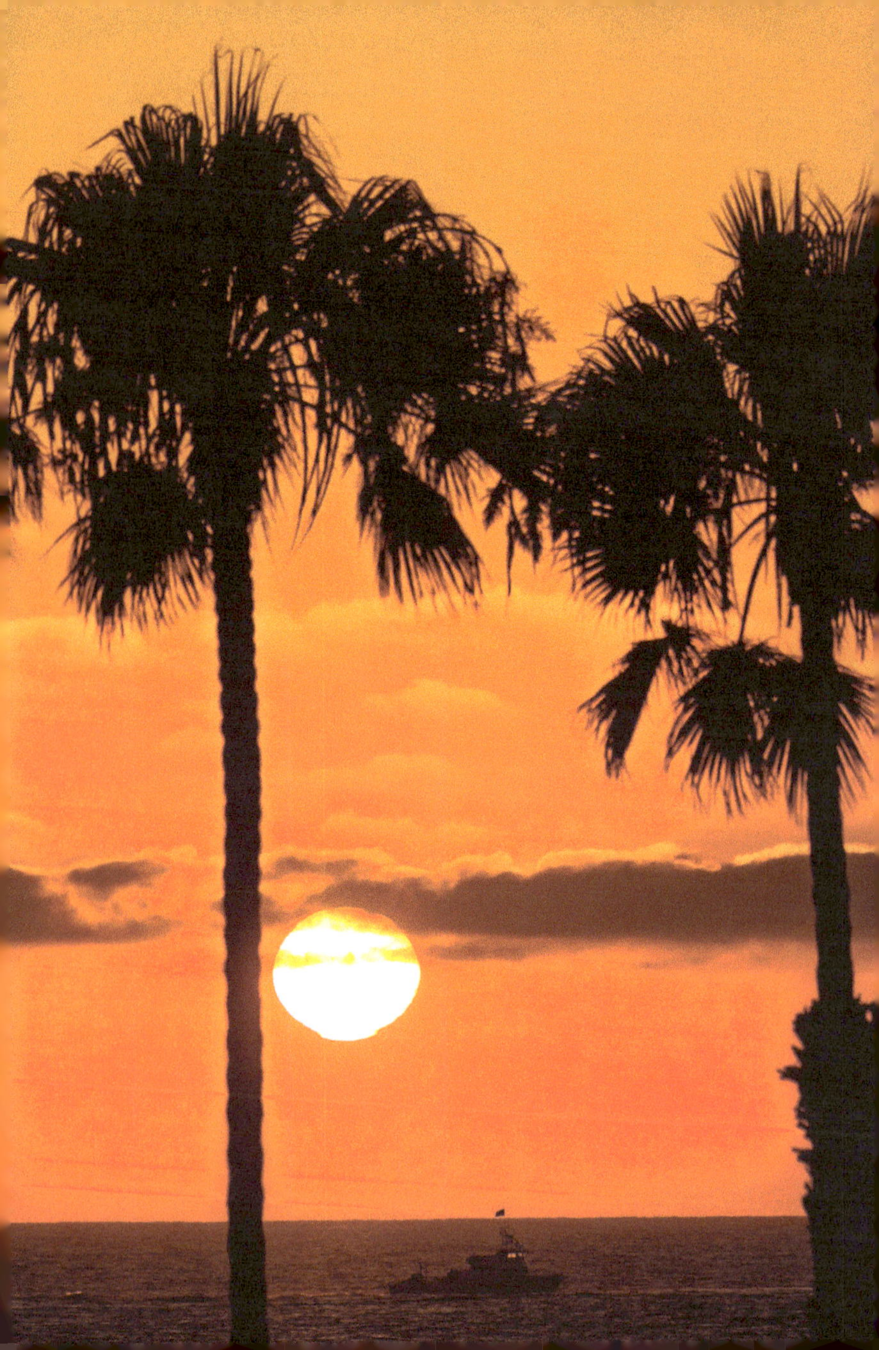

Love Heals

No pain is so deep love cannot heal. No mountain too high, no distance too far.

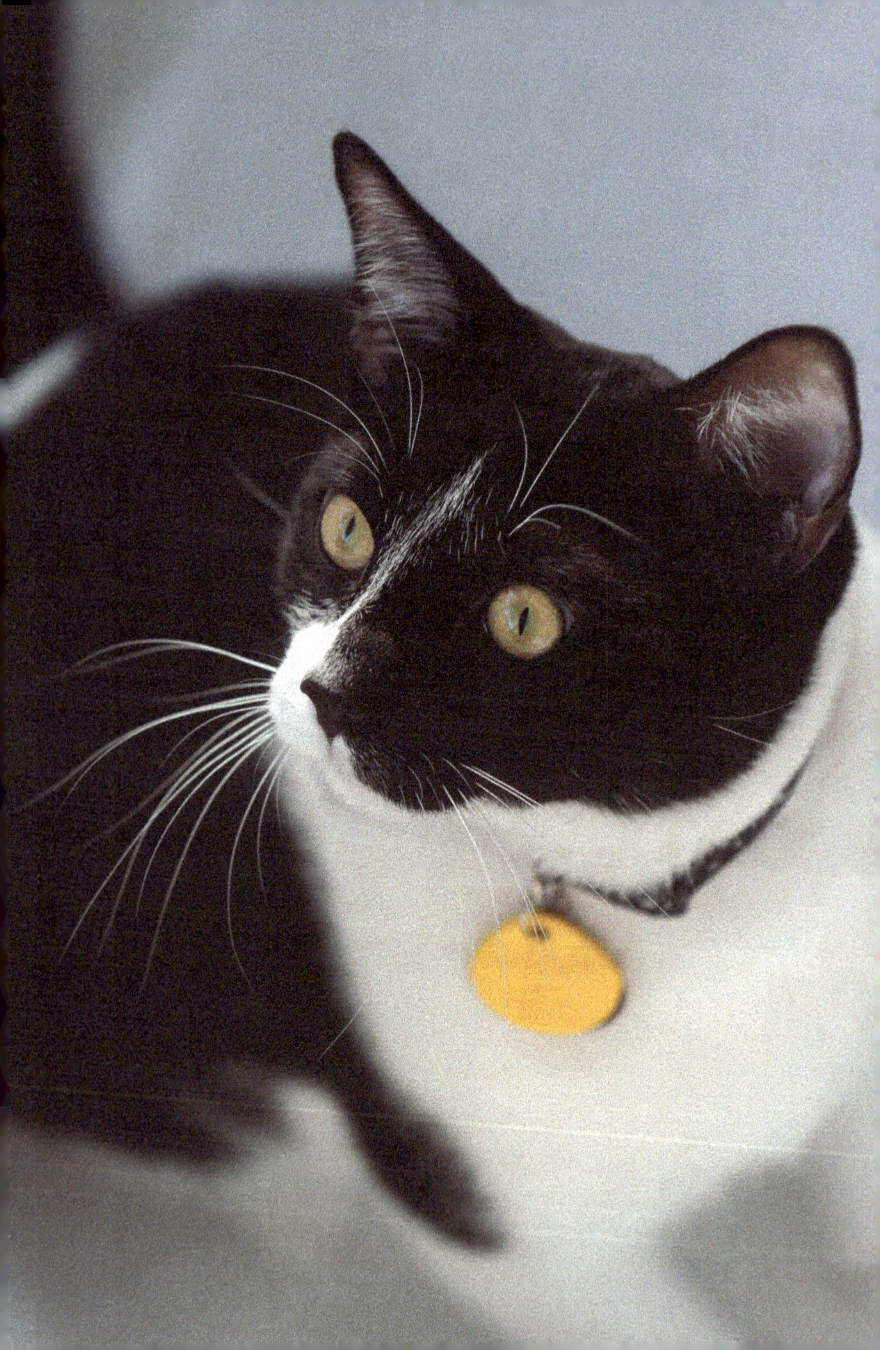

Experience Truth

The truth resonates differently than anything that is other than the truth. Today, touch the truth you hold within your heart. Be of and about this truth. Say words that deeply connect with your truth. Notice if you are going to say something that is other than your truth - and reverse directions back into your truth, beauty, all that is good, and all that is complete perfection. Your truth is this.

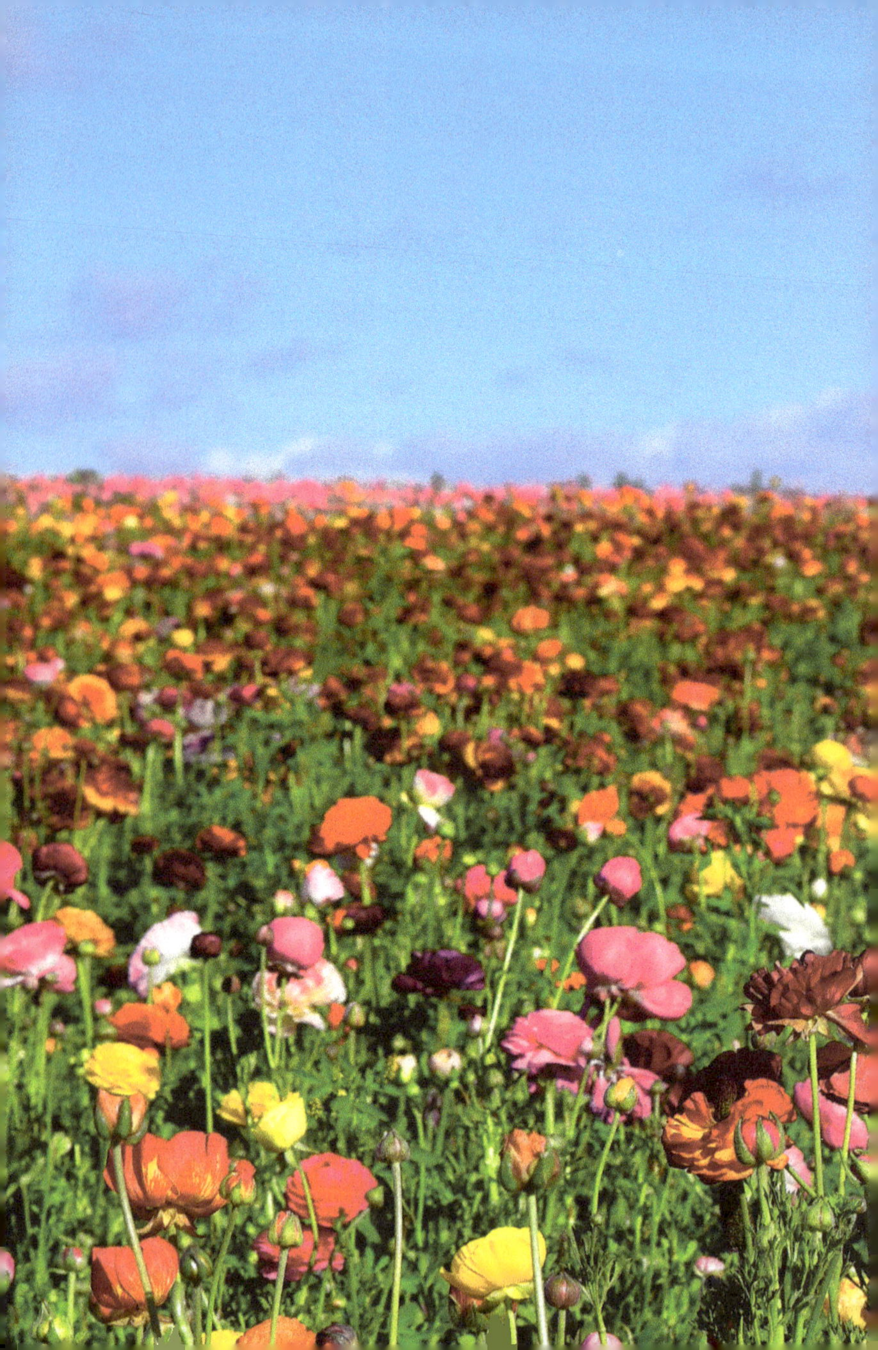

All is Beauty

Today, build your day with beauty. What if everything except beauty was an illusion? What if beauty were inherent in everything?

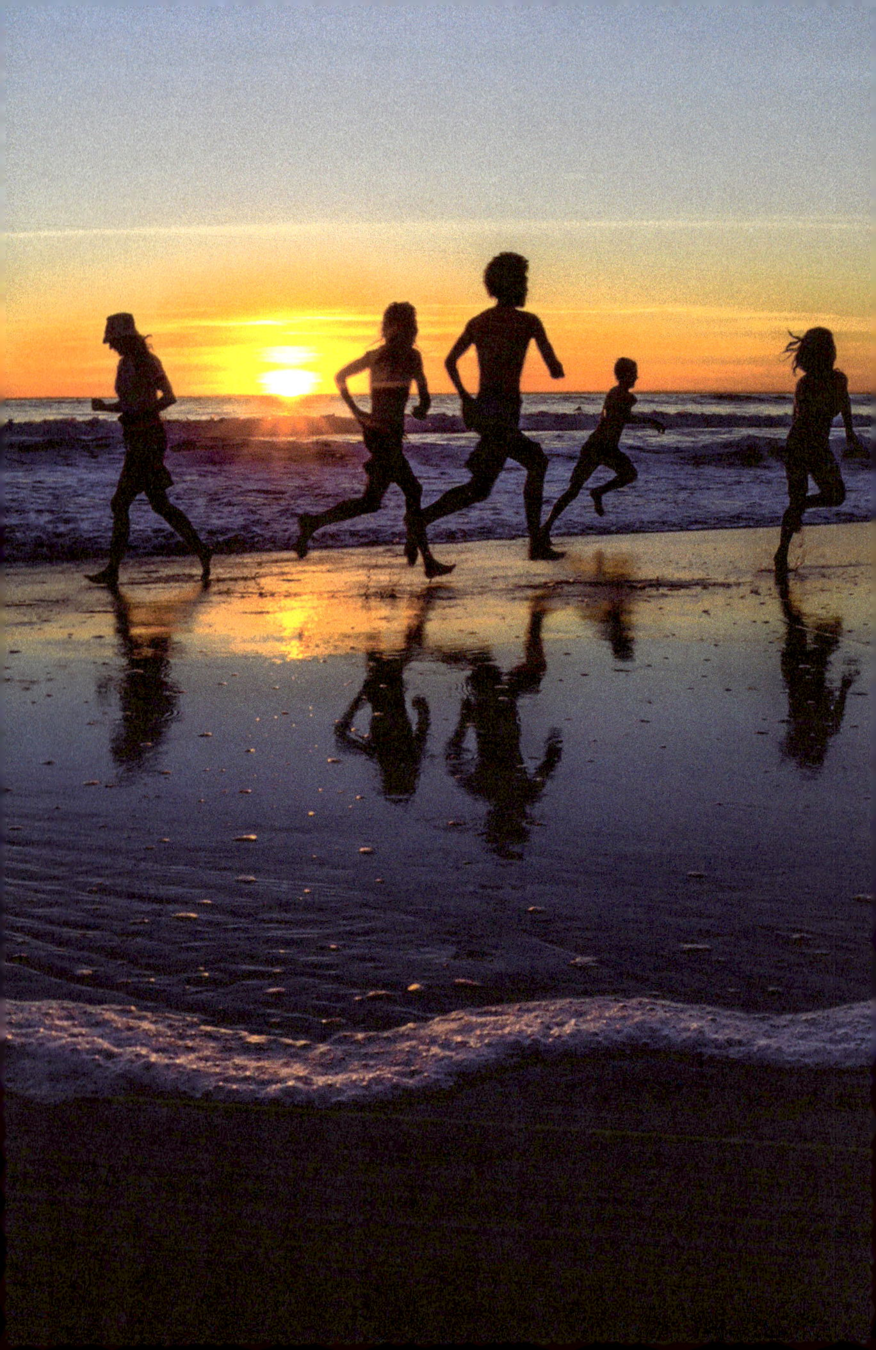

Sing it Loud

Sing loudly! Sing your song loud and wild today.

Be full of you until you are brimming over!

Express the exceptional of you.

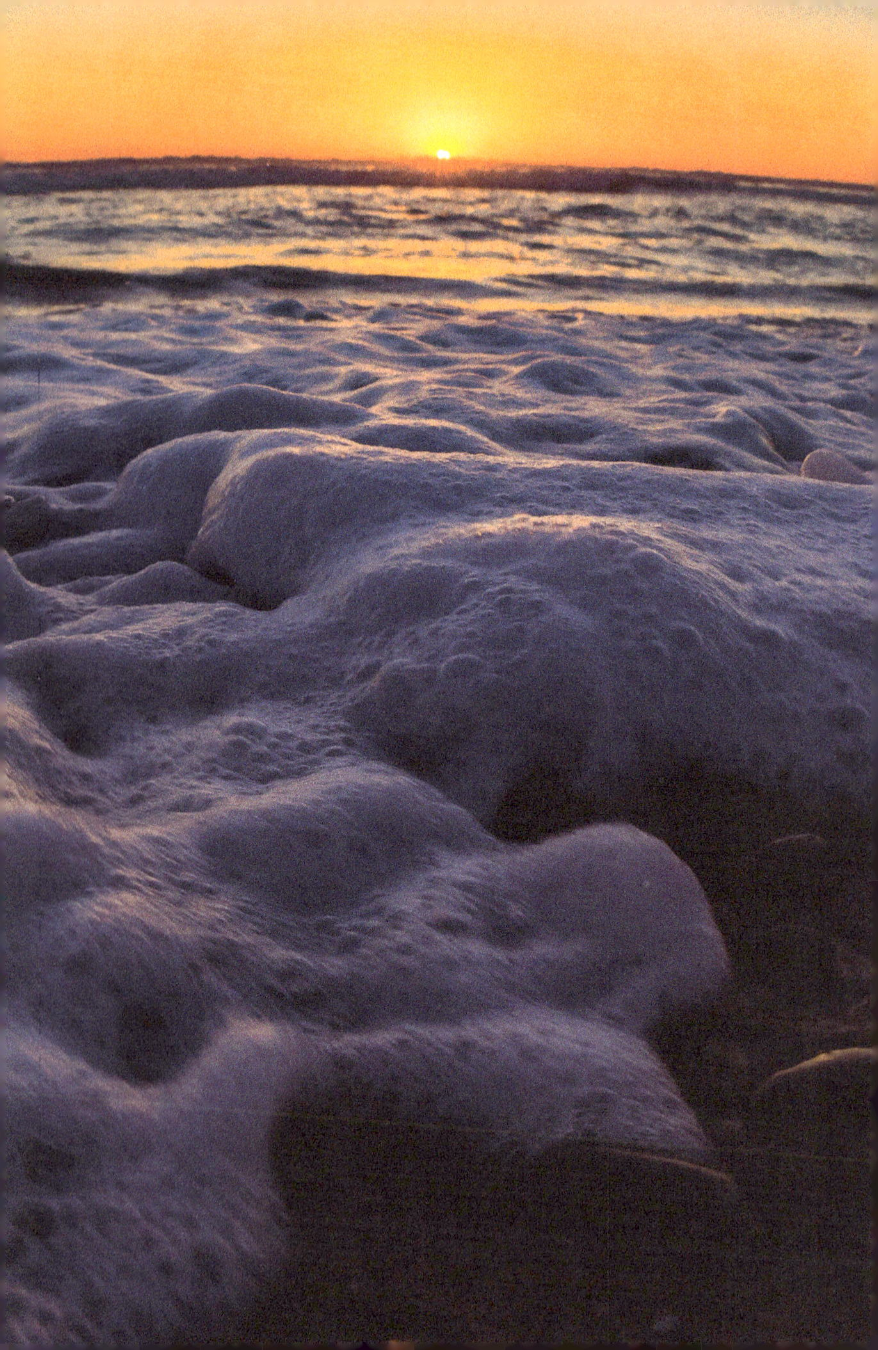

Depths of Joy

Give yourself space to experience the depths of your joy, let go of the depths of your sorrow. We are all here on this planet together at this time, in this space, see if you can reach for your dreams again.

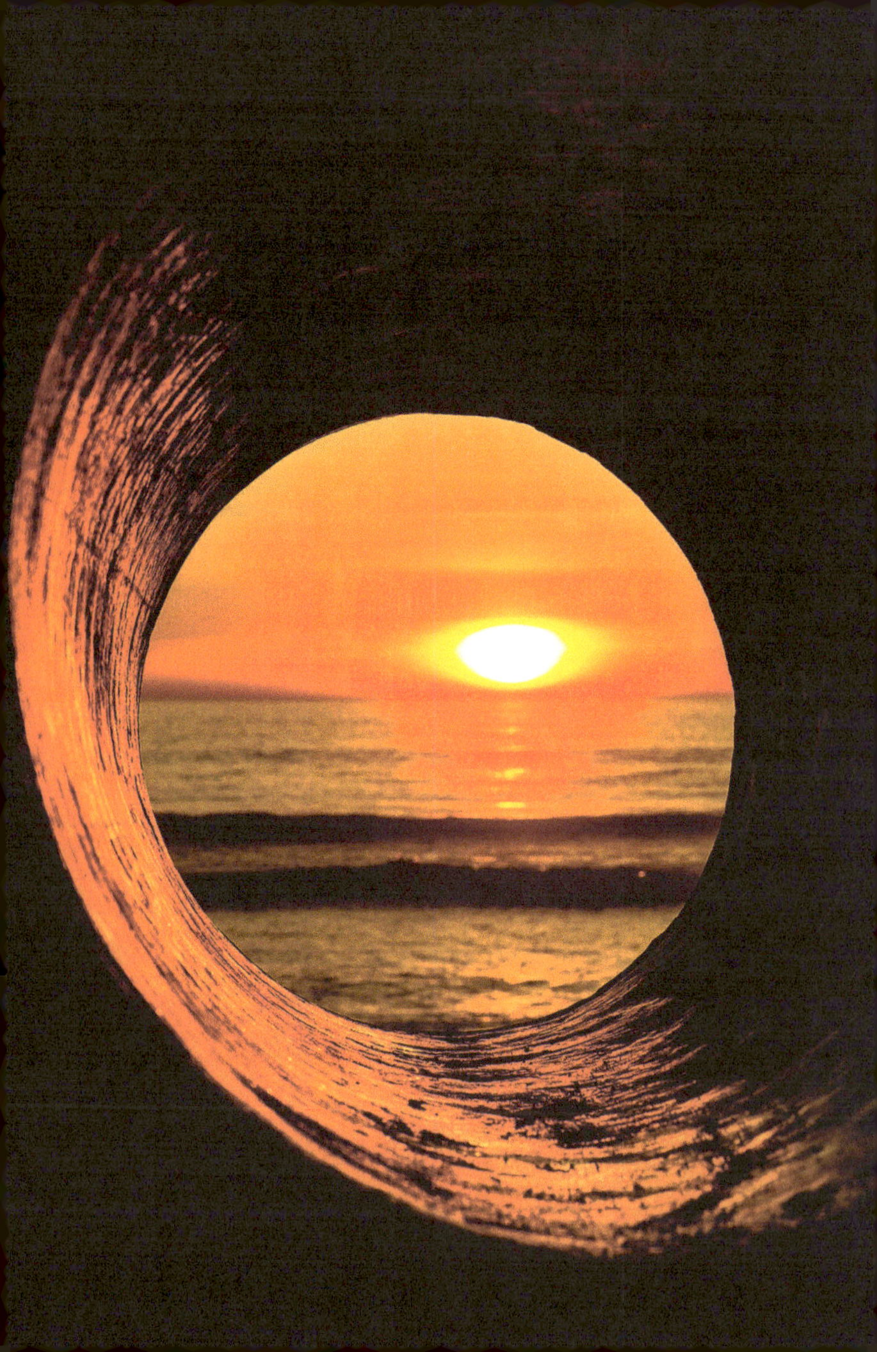

Darkness is Dispelled by Light

Light displaces darkness. Light shines, and so it is. In this beauty we are all one - beings of light.

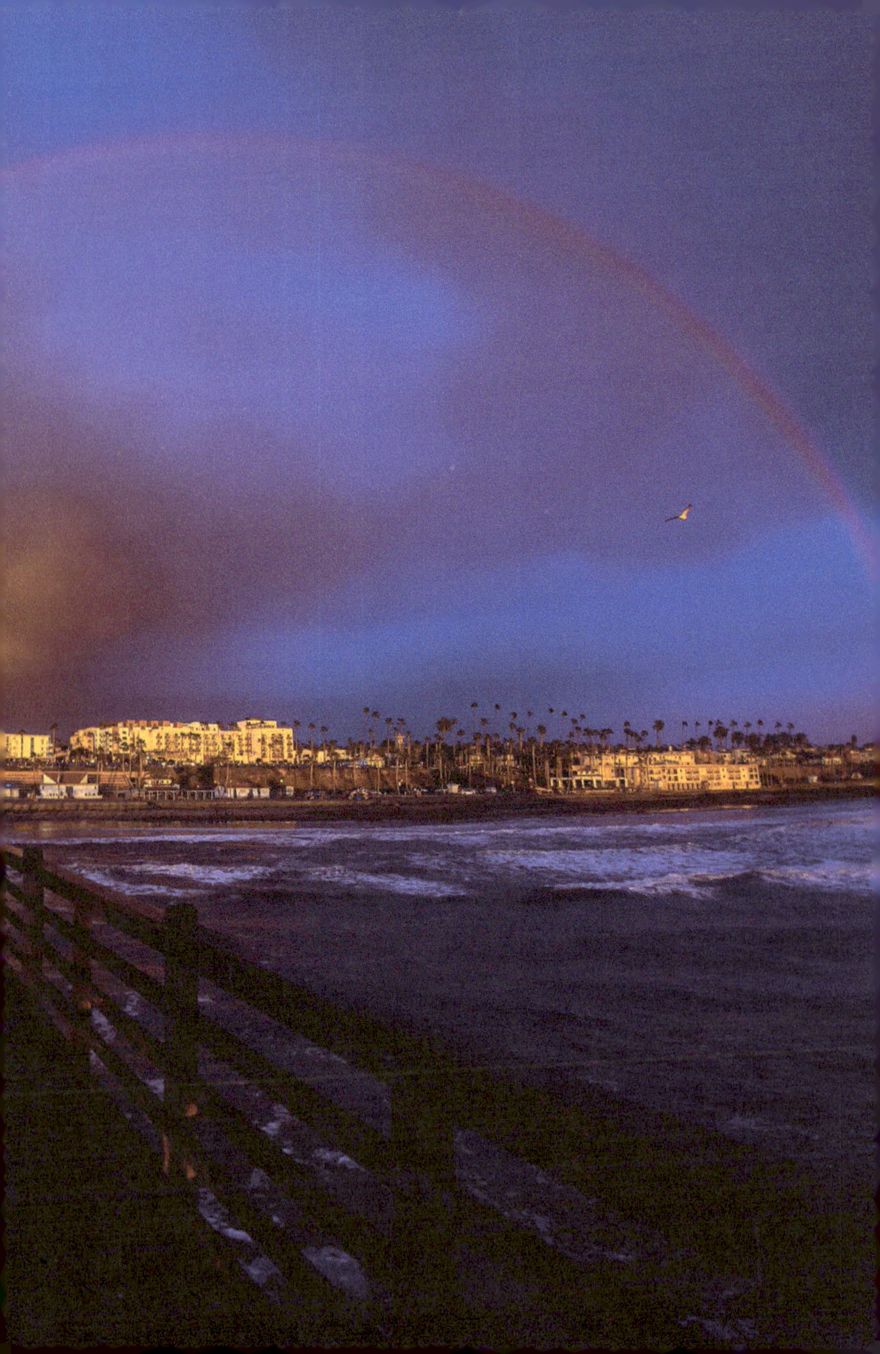

Rainbow of Glory

Allow the rainbow to shine, bringing light after darkness. It is a spark meant to awaken, will you let it in? When you cast your eyes upon something precious, allow it to change you.

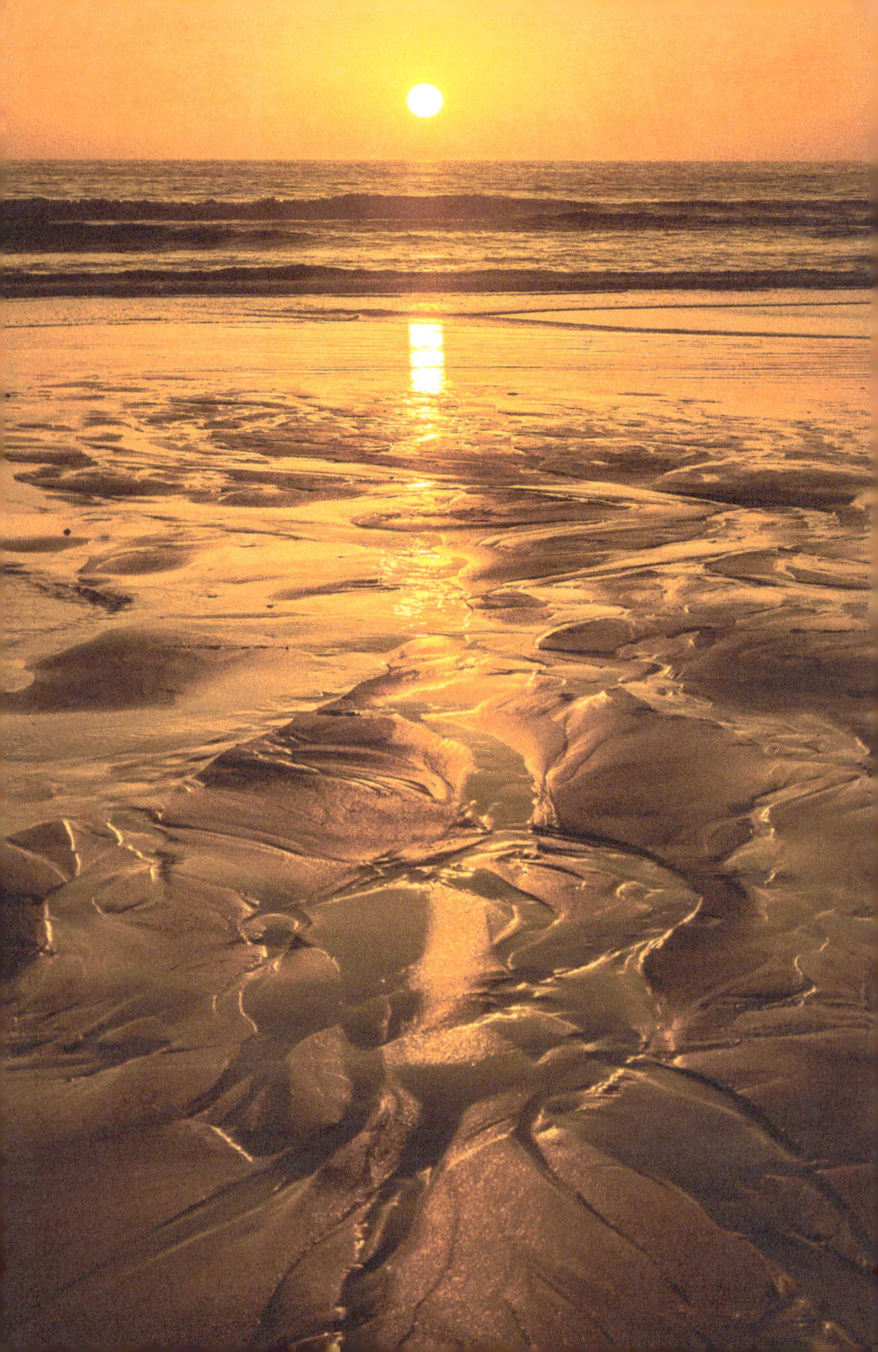

Power to Create

You have absolute power to create. Create and express the true vision of your soul. This is why you are here.

About Rich Cruse

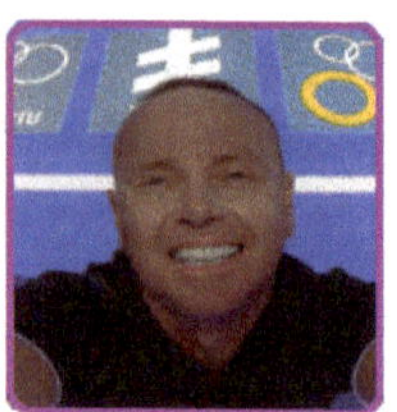

Rich Cruse sees magic and beauty everywhere he looks. A photographer for more than three decades, Rich is most at home near the ocean. He lives to photograph.
Find out more at www.CrusePhoto.com.

About Erica Marie Glessing

Erica Glessing believes when you tell your story, you change the world. She writes about happiness, joy, self-expression and more in her more than 30 books on Amazon including her favorite "Happiness Quotations: Gentle Reminders of Your Preciousness." Erica wrote over 800 original happiness quotations published first on Facebook.com/HappinessQuotations. Her passion is search engine optimization, and she runs SEOforLeadGen.com to give lightworkers on the planet tools to shine and be seen online.

If you enjoyed this book, please enjoy the other Happiness Quotations books:

Happiness Quotations: Gentle Reminders of Your Preciousness

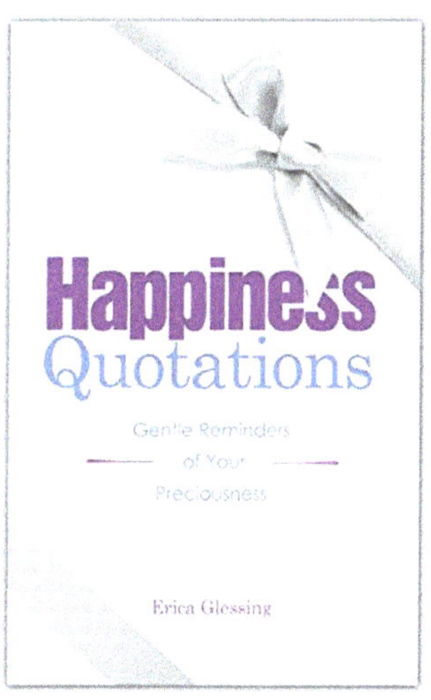

Happiness Quotations: Generative Questions to Brighten Each Day

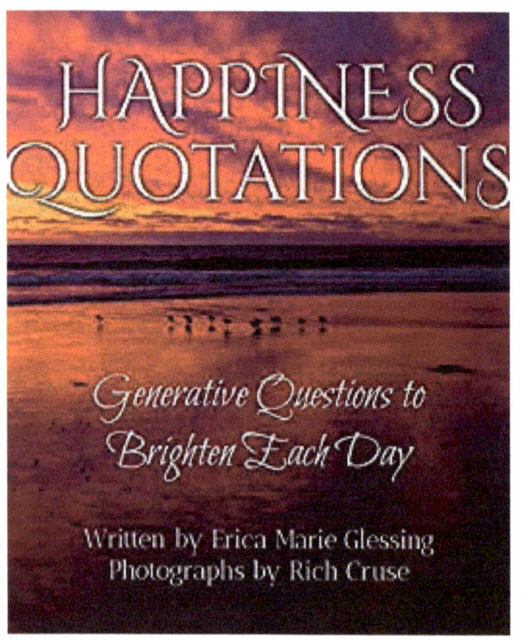

www.ingramcontent.com/pod-product-compliance
Lightning Source LLC
LaVergne TN
LVHW052349100826
845147LV00012B/790

* 9 7 8 1 6 3 6 8 4 9 1 8 8 *